Is there life on Mars?

Contents

Written by Inbali Iserles

Collins

1 Is there anybody out there?

Have you ever gazed at the sky at night
and wondered if we are alone in the universe?
Is there life on distant planets? If we look
through a **telescope** into outer space,
is someone looking back at us?
People have been searching
for answers to these kinds of
questions for thousands
of years.

What is an alien?

The word "alien" means a living creature from another planet.

Picture an alien in your mind. What does it look like? Is it like a small, green human? Is it colourful and blobby? Or spotted with a long tail? Is it whizzing around on a spaceship, a **"UFO"** (or **"unidentified flying object"**)?

Aliens are popular characters in books, films and TV shows. The most common aliens that appear in stories are "Martians" – creatures who live on the planet Mars. But do they really exist?

Life on Earth

Being "alive" is what makes animals and plants different from stuff like rocks and water. Living things grow, **reproduce** and use energy.

It is thought that life first appeared on Earth about 3.5 billion years ago. Every type of life that followed – all trees, mushrooms, birds, lizards and even humans – can be traced back to these earliest life forms.

13.8 billion years ago: universe created in big bang

3.5 billion years ago: simple life forms

230 million years ago: dinosaurs

4.5 billion years ago: our solar system formed

800 million years ago: earliest animals

Fasten your seatbelts, space travellers! We are about to set off on a journey through the solar system. Our mission is to understand what it takes for life to exist – both here, on Earth and on different planets. Lift off in three, two, one!

7 million years ago:
shared human
and chimpanzee ancestors

2 million years ago:
earliest humans

65 million years ago:
dinosaur **extinction**

4 million years ago:
oldest human ancestors

300,000 years ago:
modern humans

2 The solar system

Our solar system is made up of the Sun and eight planets. The closest planet to the Sun is Mercury. The daytime temperature there can go over 400 degrees Celsius. That's four times hotter than boiling water!

After Mercury comes Venus, Earth and Mars. Then it's the asteroid belt, where over a million huge rocks travel around the Sun. On the far side of the asteroid belt are the "gas giants": Jupiter, Saturn, Uranus and Neptune.

the solar system

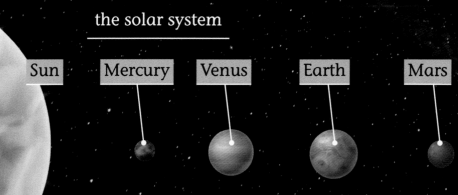

Sun   Mercury   Venus   Earth   Mars

The Sun is the largest object in our solar system.

asteroid belt

FACT! Orbiting the Sun

All the planets in the solar system travel around the Sun. Mercury takes only 88 days to complete its **orbit**. Earth's orbit takes 365 days (or a year). The furthest planet in our solar system is the huge and icy Neptune. It takes an incredible 165 years to orbit the Sun!

Jupiter   Saturn   Uranus   Neptune

What is the Sun?

The Sun is a star at the centre of our solar system. Although larger stars exist in faraway galaxies, the Sun is still absolutely gigantic.

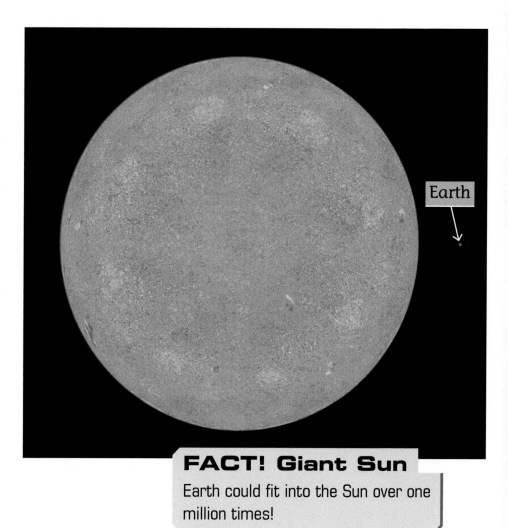

Earth

FACT! Giant Sun

Earth could fit into the Sun over one million times!

FACT! The speed of light

Earth is about 150,000,000 kilometres away from the Sun. But it only takes about eight minutes for light from the Sun to reach Earth. That's because the speed of light is the fastest speed there is (around 300,000 kilometres per second).

3 The conditions for life

So what *does* it take for life to exist? In order to survive, plants and animals (including humans) need:

- heat and sunshine (but not too much)
- air (that is safe and clean)
- water (but not too hot, or too cold).

We call these things the **"conditions for life"**. We know that planet Earth has the conditions of life – we're here to prove it! So, let's look at what this means more closely.

On Earth, forests are the "green lungs" of our planet. The trees use sunshine, gas and water to create **oxygen** – the air we need to survive.

4 Heat and sunshine

 Living things need sunshine.

Earth is lucky. As the third planet from the Sun, it gets just what it needs – enough heat for life to grow but not so much that all the water **evaporates**. If we were a lot closer to the Sun, we would boil! If we were too far away, we would freeze.

It is dangerous for a human's body temperature to climb above 40 degrees Celsius. Most animals can't live in temperatures much higher than 50 degrees Celsius.

Microbes are tiny living things that can only be seen under a **microscope**. Some are helpful, like yeast that makes bread rise. Others are known as "germs" because they can make us unwell, like the E. coli bacteria that cause tummy bugs. Many more do not help or bother us at all.

Tiny microbes live in the hot springs at Yellowstone National Park, USA.

microbes on a mobile phone

FACT! Good bacteria

Our bodies are home to around 100 trillion "good" bacteria. Many of these tiny microbes live in our gut. They help our bodies to use nutrients and keep us healthy.

Not too big, not too small

It isn't just Earth's distance from the Sun that matters, it's also the Sun's size. If the Sun was bigger, it might burn itself out. If it was too small, it wouldn't have enough **gravity** to hold the planets in a stable orbit.

As it is, our Sun is like the smallest bear's porridge in the story of *Goldilocks and the Three Bears* – it's just right!

the Milky Way

FACT! Galaxies

Scientists believe there are more than one hundred billion galaxies in the universe!

Our solar system is part of a **galaxy** called the Milky Way. A galaxy is a massive amount of gas, dust, stars and solar systems held together by gravity.

5 Air

 Living things need air.

Another important condition of life is air. Plants use the air we breathe out, together with sunlight, in order to grow.

Earth is protected by the atmosphere, a layer of gas that includes the oxygen we breathe. The atmosphere protects us from the harmful rays of the Sun and stops objects from outer space crashing into us. About once every 2,000 years, a giant meteorite breaks through the atmosphere and lands on Earth. Luckily, this is very rare.

the atmosphere

FACT! What is a meteorite?

A meteorite is a chunk of rock that comes from outer space and lands on the surface of a planet or moon.

6 Water

 Living things need water.

On Earth, we're all in luck. Over two-thirds of Earth's surface is covered in water. There is also water in the air, underground and in rivers.

Most of Earth's water is found in its huge oceans. The water evaporates and rises into clouds, then falls to Earth as rain.

FACT! Water, water everywhere!

All plants and animals on Earth contain a large amount of water. From a human to a blade of grass, everything alive on Earth is at least half water.

Earth looks blue from outer space.

7 Does Mars have the conditions for life?

We have now seen the conditions for life. We understand what makes Earth the perfect place for plants and animals (including humans) to survive. Mars is one of Earth's closest neighbours in the solar system. Does it have the conditions for life too? It's time to look at Mars more closely.

FACT! Red planet

Mars is known as the "red planet" because it looks red in the night sky. We know from **space probes** that the soil on Mars contains iron oxide. This gives the planet its colour. Iron oxide is also found in blood and rust.

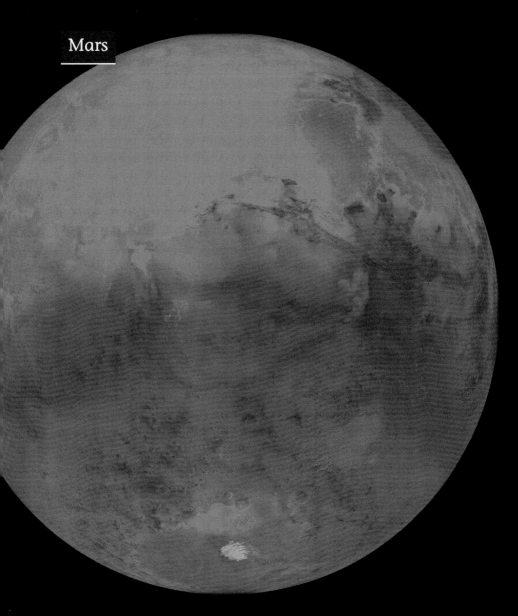

Mars

Mars is the fourth planet from the Sun. It is about half
the size of Earth, and has two small moons.

Mars takes longer than Earth to make a full journey around the Sun. A year on Earth is 365 days. A year on Mars is 687 days. So, if Martians do exist, they only have half the number of birthdays we do!

Mars has giant mountain ranges and deep valleys. Its highest mountain, Olympus Mons, is the tallest in our solar system.

FACT! Olympus Mons

Look at this artist's impression of Olympus Mons. Olympus Mons is about 25 kilometres from top to bottom. That makes it almost three times higher than Mount Everest, the tallest mountain on Earth.

Mars is named after the Roman god of war.

23

8 Is Mars too cold?

Mars is 55,000,000 kilometres
further from the Sun
than Earth, and its surface
temperature is a lot colder.
During a Martian winter,
the temperature at its poles
is a bone-chilling minus
125 degrees Celsius. That is
incredibly cold!

While Mars can get very cold,
humans have been known to
survive extreme temperatures.
A village in Siberia, Russia
recorded a winter low of almost
minus 70 degrees Celsius in 1933.
Schools there only shut when
the temperature drops below
minus 52 degrees Celsius!

a nice warm bath

shorts and
T-shirt weather

cold enough for
water to freeze

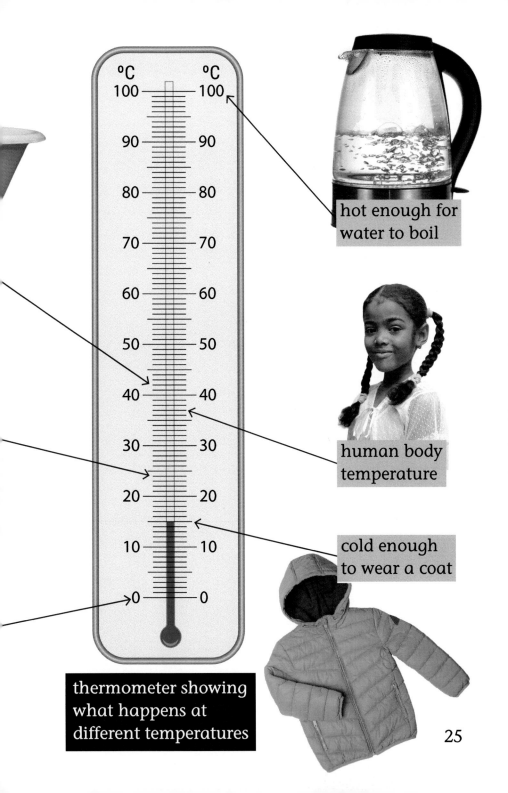

hot enough for water to boil

human body temperature

cold enough to wear a coat

thermometer showing what happens at different temperatures

25

Many creatures on Earth survive **sub-zero** conditions, such as the Arctic ground squirrel and Antarctica's Weddell seal.

The incredible red flat bark beetle has chemicals in its body that stop it from freezing – a sort of natural "antifreeze", like the kind used to stop car engines freezing. The beetle can survive temperatures as low as 150 degrees Celsius! So perhaps Mars isn't *too* cold for life to exist …

Weddell seal

red flat bark beetle

Arctic ground squirrel

Mars isn't just cold. It is windy, with jagged volcanic mountains. Life here would not be easy. But is it possible?

an artist's impression of Mars' rugged landscape

9 Lighter than air

We know that Earth has an atmosphere. This is a layer
of gas that includes oxygen, the air we breathe.
The atmosphere is like a force field that protects
the planet from sun damage. What about Mars?

an artist's impression of a
vast dust storm on Mars

Mars *does* have an atmosphere but it's a lot weaker than the one on Earth, with very little oxygen. Martian air is also full of dust. It would quickly make us ill.

FACT! Wild winds

The winds over Mars can turn into vast dust storms that rage over the planet for weeks or even months. Mars has the largest dust storms in the solar system!

Most of what we know about Mars comes from space probes. Humans have not yet landed on the red planet. The trip one way would take over half a year, and the journey would be **hazardous.**

Spacecrafts to Mars

Several spacecrafts controlled by robots have come close to Mars without touching down. For example, the European Space Agency's "Mars Express" spacecraft orbits the red planet and sends back exciting information, like the location of ice on Mars and the sort of gases that exist on the planet.

Space probes have also landed on Martian soil, such as "Perseverance", a six-wheeled robotic car from the United States and China's remote-controlled "Zhurong" rover.

space probe "Curiosity"

10 Is Mars too dry?

Mars is cold, but perhaps not too cold. It doesn't have much of an atmosphere – but it does have *some*. So how about water?

Life, as we know it, needs water to live. Let's take a closer look at the **evidence** of water on Mars.

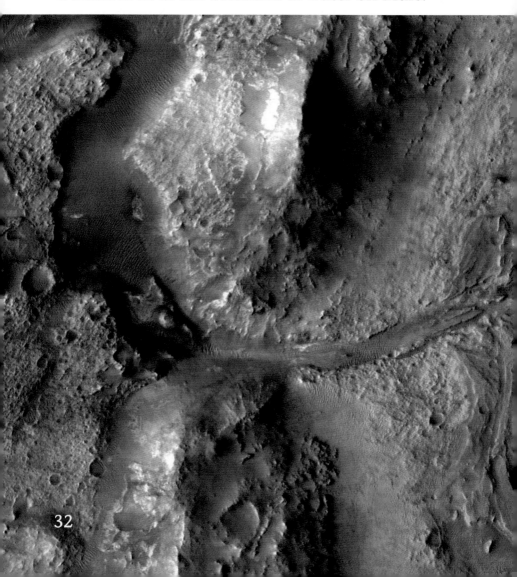

Space probe Perseverance is exploring Jezero Crater on Mars. Scientists believe that the crater was once a huge lake or sea. The probe's mission is to search the crater for **ancient** signs of life.

Was this once a river feeding into a sea?

What about today? Is there any sign that water still exists on Mars?

The answer is *possibly.* The Mars Express has discovered what looks like a group of lakes hidden under the planet's frozen surface. There is no evidence of "complex" life, like the plants and animals found on Earth. Could tiny microbes survive in the lakes – or is it too salty? Many creatures on Earth live in salty seas. But can anything live in extremely salty water?

FACT! Too salty for fish?

Studies in Earth's Dead Sea – a very salty lake between Israel and Jordan – found that microbes live there. So while hidden lakes on Mars may be too salty for fish, they may not be too salty for all life!

salt crystals on the shores of the Dead Sea

11 Other evidence of life

A Martian meteorite that landed on Earth caused excitement when scientists said that it contained tiny **fossils**. The meteorite was formed billions of years ago. It was probably launched into outer space when an asteroid hit Mars.

Martian meteorite: are those tiny fossils?

The patterns on the Martian meteorite are interesting, but most scientists do not think that they show clear evidence of ancient life.

the meteorite under a microscope

FACT! Light year

A light year is the distance that light can travel in a year, approximately nine trillion kilometres! Light moves faster than anything else in the universe.

What's that out there?

For 60 years, scientists have been looking out for signals coming from outer space. They hope to spot something unusual – a call, a message, or some other sign of alien life.

Messages from space may have to travel millions of kilometres in order to reach Earth and may arrive years later.

Scientists "listening" to space have made some exciting discoveries, like the existence of spinning "pulsar" stars that seem to blink on and off. But they have not yet found signs of alien life.

pulsar star

12 UFOs and beyond

Over the years, hundreds of people have said they have seen UFOs in the skies above Earth. It's exciting to imagine aliens floating over our heads. But there is no clear evidence that UFOs are real. People are more likely to be seeing things like Chinese lanterns, jet planes or unusual clouds.

What does all this tell us?

Although tiny microbes *may* live in hidden lakes on Mars, we have found that the planet's tough environment is not a good home for "complex" life like the plants and animals found on Earth.

Life as we know it

As we have seen, life on Earth needs heat, air and water to survive. But what if this isn't true in other parts of the universe? Could some form of life exist without sunshine? Without oxygen, or water?

41

Do not lose hope, space travellers! While complex alien life may not exist on Mars, it may exist somewhere in this vast, expanding universe.

- In the Milky Way alone, there are at least 3,200 stars orbited by planets. Could one of these planets have the conditions for life?

- Scientists believe there are at least 100 billion galaxies in the universe. Do aliens live in an unexplored galaxy?

Scientists have recently spotted "Kepler-1649c", a planet that looks like Earth in a solar system 300 light years away. The planet is about the same size as Earth, and roughly the same distance from the star it orbits as Earth is from the Sun. This means it probably has plenty of light and heat, and perhaps water and an atmosphere too.

A glimpse of this mysterious world gives us hope that the conditions for life exist there, and on many other distant planets that have not yet been discovered.

an artist's illustration of Kepler-1649c

Glossary

ancient very old

conditions for life the things life needs to survive – air that is safe to breathe, water and heat

evaporates When water evaporates, it changes into steam.

evidence anything you see, read or are told which gives you reason to believe something is true or not

extinction when a type of animal or plant dies out

fossils the ancient remains of an animal or plant that are found inside a rock

galaxy a large group of stars and planets in space that are held together by gravity

gravity the force that makes things fall when you drop them

hazardous dangerous

microscope a piece of equipment that makes it possible to see objects that are too small to see without it

orbit If something orbits the Sun, it travels around it.

oxygen a gas that forms part of the air we breathe

reproduce When animals – including people – reproduce, they produce young. When plants reproduce, they produce new plants.

space probes robotic spacecraft that travel through space to collect scientific information

sub-zero temperatures below zero degrees Celsius, the temperature at which water freezes

telescope a piece of equipment that makes objects that are faraway look nearer and larger

"UFO" or unidentified flying object an unexplained object in the sky that some people think is an alien spacecraft

Index

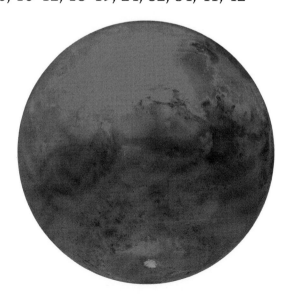

The conditions for life

What does plant and animal life need to exist?

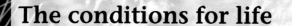

Air (that is safe and clean)

Animals need good air to breathe. Plants use the air we breathe out, together with sunlight, in order to grow.

Water (but not too hot, or too cold)

Plants and animals (including humans) need water to survive. Everything alive on Earth is at least half water.

Heat and sunshine (but not too much)

Living things need sunshine. On Earth, we are lucky: we get enough heat from the Sun for life to grow but not so much that all water evaporates.

Ideas for reading

Written by Christine Whitney
Primary Literacy Consultant

Reading objectives:
- be introduced to non-fiction books that are structured in different ways
- listen to, discuss and express views about non-fiction
- retrieve and record information from non-fiction
- discuss and clarify the meanings of words

Spoken language objectives:
- participate in discussion
- speculate, hypothesise, imagine and explore ideas through talk
- ask relevant questions

Curriculum links: Science: Basic needs of humans for survival (water, food and air); Writing: Write for different purposes

Word count: 3019

Interest words: conditions for life, evidence, hazardous, UFO, galaxy, alien

Resources: paper, pencils and crayons, access to the internet

Build a context for reading

- Ask children to discuss whether or not *aliens* exist.
- Before the children see the book, ask them what they already know about the planets that surround our sun. Can they name any of them? It may be useful to have an illustration of our solar system to support the discussion.
- Now turn to the book and read the blurb on the back cover. Ask children what they predict they will learn from this book.
- Introduce the words *evidence, hazardous, galaxy*. Ask children to work in pairs to suggest a sentence which uses one of these words correctly.

Understand and apply reading strategies

- Turn to the contents page and read through the different sections in the book. Ask for volunteers to say which section they are most interested in reading and why.
- Read together pages 2–9. Challenge children to summarise new facts they now know about life on Earth, the solar system or the Sun.